MODERN PUBLISHING'S
BEVERLY HILLS,
90210
SCRAPBOOK

by
Gio di Tazza

Modern Publishing
A Division of Unisystems, Inc.
New York, New York 10022

Printed in the U.S.A.

PHOTO CREDITS: Pages 14, 44 Movie Star News; pages 29, 30, 54 Janet Macoska; page 13 Smeal/Galella; page 17 Albert Ortega/Galella, Ltd.; page 34 Bob Scott/Galella, Ltd.; pages 28, 61 Robin Platzer/Twin Images; page 16 Mark Sennet/Onyx; page 23 Barry King/Gamma Liaison; page 38 Shahn Kermani/Gamma Liaison; page 12 Lori Stoll/Retna; page 42 Michael Benabib/Retna; page 25 Sunny Bak/Shooting Star; page 40 Ken Sax/Shooting Star; pages 47 and 49 Christopher Voelker/Shooting Star; Front cover, back cover, title page and pages 4-5, 7, 9, 10, 18, 21 (bottom), 33, 50 © Fox Broadcasting Company; pages 20 (top), 37, 56, 57, 58-59 © Bob Villard/Access Archive; pages 20 (bottom), 21 (top) New World Pictures

Cover and Interior Book Design by: Bob Feldgus

Book Number: 10625
ISBN Number: 1-56144-125-2

CONTENTS

The "Beverly Hills, 90210" cast is side by side for a sizzling second season!

INTRODUCTION

Are you hip to the zip: 90210? If you are, then settle back and get the whole scoop about one of the most popular shows on television. Lots of teens all over the world are tuning in to every episode of "Beverly Hills, 90210." It's a series that teens can relate to because it deals with relevant issues. From parental problems to dating woes, the students at West Beverly High are going through it all! The success of the show is due in part to its realism.

Another aspect that makes "Beverly Hills, 90210" irresistible is the gorgeous cast: Jason Priestley, Luke Perry, Shannen Doherty, Jennie Garth, Gabrielle Carteris, Tori Spelling, Ian Ziering, Brian Austin Green and Douglas Emerson. Are you in love with Jason or Luke? Do you admire Shannen or one of the other "90210" gals? How well do you know the characters Brenda and Brandon Walsh? Now's your chance to find out! Read on and get tantalizing tidbits of info about the characters on "Beverly Hills, 90210," and the actors who play them!

"Beverly Hills, 90210" is a huge hit not only in the United States, but in the U.K. as well. In fact, the "90210" cast recently zipped over to England to do a promo tour. Teens all over the world are hip to the zip! One thing's for sure—expect to see "Beverly Hills, 90210" on your TV set for some time to come.

Just one big, happy family ... that's the cast of "Beverly Hills, 90210"!

CHAPTER 1
THE "BEVERLY HILLS, 90210" STORY

THE WALSHES MAKE THE MOVE

Everything is going great in Minnesota for the wholesome Walsh family. That is until Jim and Cindy Walsh are told that Jim is being transferred from the Minneapolis branch of the accounting firm he works for to the company's Los Angeles office. The news doesn't sit very well with their teenage twins, Brandon and Brenda. The kids don't want to leave their friends. These are supposed to be the best years of their lives—not the years to be transplanted into a new school all the way across the country. No matter how much the kids protest, Dad and Mom say there is no alternative. So, Brenda and Brandon bid their pals farewell and pack their bags for a place called Beverly Hills.

SETTLING IN

After the first few weeks of school, Brenda and Brandon start getting acquainted with their new lives. Brenda notices that there are quite a few hunky guys at West Beverly High and Brandon finds solace in joining the school newspaper staff. After Brenda meets popular Kelly Taylor and Donna Martin, she decides she wants to be in their clique. That's not so easy because Kelly

The Walshes—the first family of TV drama!

and Donna are a tad snobby. "Bren" doesn't seem all that hip to them, or to herself either. Brenda wants to impress her new acquaintances, but she quickly learns it's silly to pretend you're something that you're not. Brenda becomes more comfortable in her new surroundings, when she realizes it's okay to be herself. Kelly and Donna like Bren's different point of view and soon they become inseparable.

At first, Brandon's life seems pretty boring. He just can't find anyone who has any depth beyond the clothes and sneakers they're wearing. Then, Brandon meets Dylan McKay, a cool cat who comes to the new kid's defense. After that, Dylan and Brandon become good friends. Brandon also develops relationships with

9

Do you know your "90210" cast? L-R: Ian Ziering, Jennie Garth, Luke Perry, Gabrielle Carteris, Shannen Doherty, Douglas Emerson, Jason Priestley, Tori Spelling, Brian Austin Green.

Kelly's ex-boyfriend, Steve "Mr. Popular" Sanders, and the sometimes-overbearing editor of the school newspaper, Andrea Zuckerman. It doesn't take level-headed Brandon too long to realize that Andrea is cool, it's just that she is struggling extra-hard to keep up her grades. The only way she can go to college is via a scholarship, so Andrea's always giving 110 percent. Brandon grows to admire her strong will and the two eventually develop a special friendship.

Brandon is also working hard. He decides to take a job working the counter at a local hangout called The Peach Pit. It's hard work, but Brandon manages his busy schedule with flying colors. In the end, the Walshes take a liking to the fantastic weather and the interesting people of California. In fact, when Jim's accounting firm offers him a chance to move back to Minneapolis months later, Cindy, Brandon and Brenda don't want to move back! Home, sweet home for the Walshes is Beverly Hills.

CHAPTER 2

MEET THE COOL CAST

JASON PRIESTLEY

ALL ABOUT BRANDON When Brandon Walsh steps into the luxurious lifestyle of Beverly Hills, it's as if he's walking into a dream. He encounters many things he never found back in the Midwest. At first, many of the students at West Beverly Hills High pegged Brandon as a wide-eyed, naive, new kid. He was, to a degree. But Brandon is a fast learner and pretty soon, he finds his niche. He starts working on the school paper and hanging out with the coolest kid around—Dylan.

Brandon's a normal guy thrust into a seemingly glamorous, fast-paced Beverly Hills lifestyle, but he's secure enough with who he is that he won't let go of his Midwestern values and morals.

ACT I Take one look at Jason Priestley's shimmering eyes and it's not hard to take an instant liking to this Canadian-born actor. Jason was born on August 28th in Vancouver, British Columbia. Now Jason lives in California though his family still lives in Canada. Jason admits that he gets homesick sometimes.

Originally from Vancouver, Jason has found a new home in the hearts of millions of fans worldwide.

"Yes, I do miss my family," he says. "Vancouver is such a beautiful place, it's easy to miss!"

Jason's acting career started when "J" (that's what his close pals call him) was a four-year-old tyke. Jason was watching TV and decided that he could do what all those kids on TV were doing—act. Even then, Jason's determination and conviction were evident. J bopped over to his mother and told her his plans. Jason's mother, a dancer/actress/choreographer/singer, knew how tough the rejection is, so she hesitated.

"I asked my mom if I could do it and she kind of balked at me," recalls J. "She kind of said, 'Well, I don't know.' Then I asked her again and she said it was okay. She was very cool about it. She wasn't a stage mother whatsoever. She actually used to make me pay her to drive me to my auditions. I said, 'Why do I have to pay you?' And she said, 'Well, if I didn't drive you, you'd have to pay the cabdriver.' She was very cool."

After J got the green light from his mom, he went after his dream full force ahead. Jason's mom took him to her agent and Jason started working almost immediately in commercials. By the age of eight, Jason had already starred in his first made-for-television movie, "Stacey," for the Canadian Broadcasting Company. At the age of 12, Jason came to an important decision: He decided he wanted to stop acting.

Triple-threats Jason Priestley, Shannen Doherty and Luke Perry were presenters at the 43rd Annual Emmy Awards show.

"I quit because it didn't seem right to me," remembers Jason. "I was about 12 and I just didn't want to worry about whether my tooth got chipped. I looked at a lot of these child actors who are 14 and 15 years old and they can't do anything. So, I said, 'This is wrong, come on.' And I quit. Before I started acting again, I broke two of my front teeth in half, I had 13 scars on my face,

Jason as he appeared on the TV program "Sister Kate."

and I shaved all my hair off. I took some years to just be a kid—a regular kid. I got back into it in my senior year in high school." It's a good thing too, because America may have never gotten to know and love Jason as well as we do!

After Jason started acting again, his career grew to include appearances in many TV series, including "21 Jump Street," "Quantum Leap" and "Airwolf." He also appeared in the films "Watchers," "The Boy Who Could Fly" and "Nowhere To Run." Jason also found his way onstage with productions of "The Breakfast Club," "Rebel Without A Cause" and "Addict." The TV series that J starred in before "Beverly Hills, 90210" was "Sister Kate," in which he played the eldest orphan, Todd Mahaffey. He also starred opposite his good friend Robin Lively in both "Teen Angel" and "Teen Witch" for the Disney Channel.

Jason believes in giving his all when it comes to acting. He is extremely dedicated and puts a lot of pressure on himself to do his very best each and every day. A lot of times, that means getting to bed early. "I'm out of bed most mornings before the sun comes up and I don't get home until way after dark," says J. His friends buzz him and ask him to go out, but Jason often has to decline.

THE REAL DEAL Currently, Jason makes his home in Woodland Hills, California. Like most of the cast of "Beverly Hills, 90210," J doesn't have a whole lot of free time, but he does like to spend his time off playing sports. In fact, Jason plays center on a local division-two hockey team. J also enjoys perfecting his golf game. Other sports that Jason digs are motorcycling, snow skiing, tennis and rugby.

When asked if there was anything else Jason wanted to get into besides acting, you might think he would answer hockey, but that's not the case. There was a time in his life when he wanted to be a pilot.

Jason is also a big fan of books—especially mystery stories. "I like mystery writers," he says.

Wild-at-heart Jason with his favorite means of transport.

Although Jason likes acting, he's the type of person who likes to conquer new fields. That's why he sees himself directing someday. However, J makes it clear that he must first master one craft "before moving on to the next!" Whatever field that Jason decides to move on to next, he'll be a success because he's so talented.

As one of TV's top stars, Jason's always in the right place at the right time. Here, he and actress Robin Lively attend the 18th Annual Daytime Emmy Awards.

SHANNEN DOHERTY

BRENDA IN A NUTSHELL Many female fans of "Beverly Hills, 90210" can relate to Brenda Walsh like no other character on prime-time television. Why? Brenda is a typical teen who's going through the motions of growing up, fitting in and learning about herself. Brenda is Brandon's twin, who desperately wants to fit into her new posh environment while trying to keep her Midwestern ideals intact. Shannen says of Brenda's experience, "To Brenda Walsh, moving to Beverly Hills is like entering a brave new world. It's exciting, glamorous and sophisticated—like Wonderland with land mines."

No one knows Brenda better than Shannen. "Brenda started out on the show to be a very insecure girl who really would do anything to fit in with the 'in' crowd," explains Shannen. "She just wanted to be popular and she wanted to be liked. But the more the show has gone on, the more she's really come into her own. She's really become more secure with herself."

Brenda and other "Beverly Hills, 90210" characters experience peer pressure on each show. Remember when the Walshes first moved to Hillcrest Drive in Beverly

Brenda and Dylan—a heavenly match.

Hills? Brenda started hanging out with the popular clique. Kelly and Donna wanted to go out and shop. Although Brenda didn't have any money to blow on an expensive outfit, she went along. Brenda became irritable toward her parents because they were making her feel inadequate in front of new friends. That episode also dealt with shoplifting. Brenda's down-to-earth values told her shoplifting is a crime and that was that.

In terms of peer pressure, Shannen says that a poor excuse is when you say that you *had* to do something. You are in control in the end. Shannen feels that nobody ever forces you to attach to your friends and do whatever they do. Your friends can't force you to do anything that you don't want to do. She suggests that one has to get some confidence, and be secure in oneself to say, "No. I'm my own person and I'm going to do what I want to do."

IN THE BEGINNING When Shannen Doherty was growing up in Memphis, Tennessee, little did she know that she'd soon be resettling in California—just like the character she plays in "Beverly Hills, 90210"! Well, that's exactly what happened. Shannen's family moved to Southern California when she was six years old. Shannen Doherty's parents, Tom and Rosa, were not thrilled when their daughter said she wanted to get into acting. But Shannen insisted she could be successful and, finally, her parents gave in. Ten-year-old Shannen worked hard, going on audition after audition. She learned to deal with rejection and eventually, all her determination paid off. Shannen's first television appearance was a two-part episode of "Father Murphy." A year later, Shannen was cast by the late Michael Landon to play the role of Jenny Wilder in the NBC series "Little House: A New Beginning."

Shannen gets very sentimental and emotional when she thinks about Michael Landon. She considered him as her mentor, and she misses him deeply.

After her "Little House: A New Beginning" role, Shannen landed the part of Kris Witherspoon on the NBC family drama "Our House." Her extensive list of TV guest-starring credits includes appearances on such shows as "21 Jump Street," "Life Goes On," "Magnum, P.I.," "The Outlaws," "Airwolf" and "The Voyagers." And that's not all! She also starred with Lindsay Wagner and Jack Scalia in the made-for-television movie "The Other Lover," and with Brad Davis and Jack Warden in the television mini-series "Robert Kennedy and His Times," and in the feature film "Girls Just Want To Have Fun." Shannen also made appearances in "The Treasure of

Shannen's many faces…!

in "Little House:
A New Beginning"

in "Heathers"

in "Girls Just Want To Have Fun"

in "Beverly Hills, 90210" with co-stars Jennie Garth and Tori Spelling

Green Pinney" and "Night Shift." You probably remember Shannen from the dark comedy "Heathers," in
which she starred as Heather Duke opposite Christian
Slater and Winona Ryder. Shannen says she enjoyed
working with Christian and Winona and thinks they're
fabulous actors. The three still keep in touch.

Acting is more than just a job for 20-year-old Shannen.
She enjoys all aspects of acting and she's happy with
the opportunities that she's had.

THE SHANNEN SCOOP In her free time, Shannen enjoys
playing tennis, horseback riding, snow skiing and exer-
cising. Although her "Beverly Hills, 90210" character is
a bit of a shopaholic, Shannen isn't addicted to the
words "Charge it!" In fact, Shannen would prefer to
spend an evening reading a good book or making some
homemade pasta. Shannen's dad is a gourmet chef and
he taught her quite a bit about cooking. Shannen's favorite smell of all is the smell of garlic in olive oil and
butter. Sounds delicious!

Although it's easy for fans to imagine that Shannen's
life is overflowing with glitzy parties and lots of fun,
the truth is quite different. Shannen says there are
plenty of nights she spends alone eating in her apart-
ment with her dogs, memorizing her lines until the wee
hours. Even if she had loads of time, Shannen isn't the
type of person who likes to go "clubbing."

When asked about dating Jason or Luke, Shannen
admits that the two dudes are hunk material. One ques-
tion that she's always bombarded with is: What's it like
playing Luke Perry's girlfriend? Since Luke and Shannen play boyfriend and girlfriend on the show, they do
have to kiss all the time. But with about 40 people watching!

So, who's the man in Shannen's life? He's a 25-year-old
real estate developer. Although marriage isn't in her
immediate plans, Shannen does say that her beau is
simply dreamy!

When she's not hanging out with her friends, Shannen

Catch rising star Shannen Doherty in 1988!

is chilling with man's best friend or a good book. "I love
to read," says Shannen. "I love taking my three dogs to
the park and I love horseback riding, so I go riding a
lot. Also, I have a lot of friends who are musicians and
writers and they're very mellow people." So, when Shannen goes out with her "mellow" pals, they usually end
up at a place that has good music. However, it's also

important that the music isn't too loud, so they can all just kick back and talk, which Shannen loves to do!

One of Shannen's closest chums is co-star Tori Spelling. "Tori's one of my best friends!" exclaims Shannen. "We see each other like every single night. We're really close!"

When asked to describe herself, Shannen uses a string of adjectives. "Confident, mellow, ambitious, fun, and very normal," offers the brunette actress. "Very, very, very normal." Does candid Shannen have any secrets that she can share with you? Sure! "I'm scared of horror films," she says. "I can't see them because I'll have nightmares for two weeks!"

Shannen is by nature a very caring person. She adores animals and has been known to adopt as many as 15 dogs at a time from the local animal shelter and then proceeds to find homes for them. It is very important to Shannen that she make her contribution to society. That's why she also spends some of her free time counseling teens about alcoholism and drugs. She works with the Just Say No campaign and with MacLaren Hall, a center for abused children. Her extensive work with the American Lung Association prompted the association to donate $100,000 to medical research in Shannen's name. Way to go, Shannen!

LUKE PERRY

DYLAN'S DEAL If you're a fan of Dylan McKay, then you probably already know that he's the coolest cat at West Beverly Hills High. Remember when, early in the series, Dylan befriended the "new kid"—otherwise known as Brandon Walsh? Dylan is above peer pressure and has a lot more depth than many of the shallow socialites that attend West Beverly Hills High. He likes classical literature, music and art.

Believe it or not, Luke didn't always want to play the part of Dylan! "I made it very clear that I wasn't interested in playing a high school hood," reveals Luke.

"But when they explained other aspects of the character, I came out excited—which is nice."

Needless to say, Luke really enjoys playing Dylan McKay. "I love my character because he's so intelligent," says Luke. "There's a scene where Dylan stops these bullies from beating up a freshman without ever taking his hands out of his pockets. That's intimidation through intelligence."

Luscious Luke's good looks drive fans wild.

Is Dylan somebody Luke would be friends with? "Dylan is the type of guy I would want as a friend—you know, independent and intelligent," explains Luke, "very much a free spirit. I like that. Dylan has a sense of what's right and wrong. A lot of people coming from Dylan's advantageous background forget what's right and wrong—they only think about what they can afford, but he remembers and I dig that."

When asked if Luke and Dylan are similar in some ways, Luke thinks for a moment before answering. "I seem to be lacking a 1963 Porsche," he says with a chuckle. "That's one of the more upsetting differences between Dylan and Luke. But seriously, I didn't grow up rich like he did. I didn't have a lot of money. Dylan's pretty angry, rebellious. I'm not like that. I'm a pretty happy guy, I think."

As Luke points out, although Dylan may act like everything is peachy keen, he does have some problems. Dylan's mother left him 11 years ago and he has trouble dealing with that fact. A recent episode of "Beverly Hills, 90210" explored this aspect of Dylan's personality when his mom re-enters his life. The emotional shock of it all leads Dylan to drink. Dylan may act as if he's happy being a loner and that everything is okay, but under it all there's a lot of pain and plenty of secrets. In fact, it is this mysterious quality that drives many of the gals at West Beverly Hills High absolutely mad about Dylan McKay!

LIFE ACCORDING TO LUKE Brown-eyed Luke Perry was born on October 11 in Mansfield, Ohio. He grew up in Fredericktown, Ohio, a town which he describes as being a small farming town.

Luke told Arsenio Hall with a playful smile in a recent interview that he lived on a farm, pitching hay and looking after the cows and sheep.

High school was the source of a lot of frustration for Luke. He didn't like the fact that he wasn't treated like an adult. Asked if he performed in high school plays, he replies with a snort, "I was kicked out of the school play! I said, 'That's it for you guys. I'm not acting here anymore!' I didn't do anymore school plays and I came to Los Angeles right after graduation."

After high school, Luke moved to Hollywood with a few dollars in his pocket and a dream. Ever since he was little, Luke had wanted to act. "I can't remember wanting anything else!" he exclaims. He soon got his wish. Luke landed the role of Ned Bates on the daytime drama series "Loving." Luke played Ned for a year and then moved to the soap opera "Another World," playing Kenny. "Another World" is filmed in New York City, so Luke packed his bags and headed east. While in New York City, Luke decided to take advantage of all the fabulous opportunities the Big Apple has to offer. Luke studied acting with Bobby Lewis and Marcia Jean Kurtz. However, Luke considers his mentor to be his first acting teacher, David Beard, with whom he studied in Los Angeles.

It wasn't too long after his soap roles that Luke starred in his first feature film, "Terminal Bliss." He also did loads of commercials including a Levi's 501 jeans ad. That was his all-time favorite. Why? "I grew up in them," states Luke simply.

More recently, Luke starred in the feature film "Scorchers," with Faye Dunaway, James Earl Jones and Emily Lloyd. "Scorchers" is scheduled for a Christmas release in 1991. Some of the actors and actresses that Luke admires are Marlon Brando, Paul Newman, Annie Potts, Ellen Barkin, Meryl Streep, Kurt Russell and Kevin Costner.

When handsome Luke has some time to himself, he likes to play with his pot belly pig, which he named Jerry Lee after 50s rock 'n' roller Jerry Lee Lewis. "I have a big yard for him and he's a great pet!" says Luke. When it comes to music, Luke really likes rock 'n' roll, country music and opera. Two of his favorite singers aside from Jerry Lee Lewis are B.B. King and Luciano Pavarotti. Luke confesses, however, that the only place that *he* sings is in the shower! Since Luke is a real down-to-earth guy, he still keeps in touch with his

Luke and fellow "Loving" cast members played basketball to benefit the Youth at Risk cause.

friends from back home—especially his best bud, David. Luke's hometown adores him. When he went back to Fredericktown to make an appearance, 7,000 fans turned out for autographs!

Luke is a private type of guy. He likes to spend a lot of time alone, watching movies or television. In fact, Luke sees movies that he likes a few times. Some of Luke's favorite TV shows are "Starsky & Hutch," "The Rockford Files" and "Jeopardy!" His "90210" character may think that surfing is the deal, but the real Luke thinks it's just "okay." When Luke feels like getting outdoors, you might find him on the basketball court, at a quiet lake with a fishing rod in his hand, or in the sky. That's right, Luke likes skydiving! Luke also likes fencing, gymnastics, stock car racing and all water sports.

Luke realizes that he is in a position to reach thousands of teens all across America. He accepts that responsibility with open arms. In fact, at a Traffic Safety Now event during "Buckle Up America" week, Luke spoke about the importance of buckling up.

Luke thrives on action and adventure.

Luke appreciates his fans' attentions at an autograph signing in
Cleveland, Ohio.

Some call Luke the James Dean of the '90s. However, Luke just sees himself as a "fun-ish" kind of guy. "People freak out laughing when they see me," he says. Well, that's because they're so excited and nervous to see Luke in person.

If Luke couldn't act anymore, what would he do? He says that he would want to be a fireman. That's a perfect Perry answer because benevolent Luke is always thinking about how he can help those in need.

With all the hype that "Beverly Hills, 90210" is getting, and all the attention Luke is getting himself, you have to wonder what he thinks about it all. How does Luke Perry see himself? "A skinny kid from Ohio trying to do the best he can!" says Luke.

Regarding romance, Luke says that he's not permanently attached to anyone at the moment. Says Luke, "I play the field—responsibly!"

An important aspect of "Beverly Hills, 90210" according to Luke, is that it doesn't talk down to teenagers. He thinks the writing and the tackling and presentation of issues is right on. "A lot of people forget that high school kids are intelligent!" exclaims Luke. "All they remember are the zits, problems and no self-confidence. But come on! I don't think there is any other social group that is as aware as teenagers. ... You are not an adult yet; everyone thinks you should act like one—but they don't treat you like one. It's the basis for a lot of frustration."

When asked if he has any advice for all the viewers who tune into "Beverly Hills, 90210" every week, Luke responds with a laugh, "Get your homework done before you watch it, and go to bed immediately after! Just kidding! No, just watch the show, read between the lines, and see what is really going on out there. Don't be afraid to ask questions. If the show inspires something in you, don't be afraid to react to it and ask questions. Also, thanks for watching!"

We wouldn't miss an episode of "Beverly Hills, 90210" for the world!

TORI SPELLING

DONNA'S CLIQUE Donna Martin, hip clique chick of "Beverly Hills, 90210," doesn't appreciate being called stupid. The 18-year-old actress, Tori Spelling, who plays Donna couldn't agree with her more. "My character, Donna Martin, is kind of ditzy," begins Tori. "She's into money. She puts down people who aren't popular, I think she's more sensitive than that, though. I think she's really funny." Is Tori at all like Donna? "I am not like my character at all," says Tori. "She is a total snob and I am more relaxed."

Some people may automatically assume that since Tori also grew up in Hollywood, her life is similar to Donna's or Kelly's. However, Tori clears up the confusion. "People always think the show is patterned after my life," she begins. "But, not really. My life is not like that. My high school is *totally* different. I go to a private all-girls school that's really strict. I had a much more strict upbringing than the kids on the show."

TORI'S STORY Victoria Spelling is not a newcomer to the Hollywood life. She comes from a family well-rooted in the entertainment business. Tori's mom, Candy, is in the business and her dad is super-producer Aaron Spelling. Mr. Spelling even produces "Beverly Hills, 90210"! It was only natural that Tori would follow in the family's footsteps.

Tori made her motion picture debut in "Troop Beverly Hills." She has also performed in over a dozen network television productions, including appearances and co-starring roles on "Saved By The Bell," "Monsters," "The Wizard," "T.J. Hooker," "Fantasy Island" and "Hotel." Tori was also in the ABC Movie for Television "The Three Kings." In 1987, Tori was nominated for the Youth in Film best acting award.

Although it's difficult starring on "90210" and going to school at the same time, Tori somehow manages it all.

"It's hectic!" she exclaims. "During shooting I go to

Tori's role of snobby, style-conscious Donna Martin is a challenge
for this down-to-earth girl.

school about once a week. That's really hard. I get back to school and I am *totally* lost. It's really hard to keep up. So far, it's been okay. I don't have a tutor on the set because I took a proficiency exam. Technically, I've graduated from high school, but I still wanted to go because I don't want to miss out on anything and regret it."

Tori turns out with the entire Spelling clan. L-R: Tori, mom, super-producer dad Aaron Spelling and Tori's little brother.

So, what's it like growing up in Hollywood? Tori says that it's a lot of fun. "When I was younger, my dad always took me to cast parties and affairs," she remembers. "I would always meet the stars and it got me used to being around those types of people. So it was easier for me to break into the business and be more comfortable with it. Other than that, it was pretty okay. It was the same as for any other kid."

Just as lots of fans ask Shannen what it's like hanging out with the gorgeous guys of "Beverly Hills, 90210," people ask Tori the same thing. "My friends ask if I've ever gone out with them or kissed them! I'm like, 'No!!' It's weird, we are so close, I don't even think of them as gorgeous. They are just guys that I'm with every day."

Since Tori spends so much time with Jason, Luke and the other dudes on "90210," she has become very close to them all. "We get along together really well, and we're all really good friends," says Tori. "The cast is like my second family. I can talk to any of them. They give me advice and everything. I always wanted an older brother and I've never had one. It's great, now I have Jason and Luke!"

When Tori has some free time, she likes to play volleyball, go skiing and write. She also is interested in fine-tuning her acting skills. She does some private training with Kathryn Daly of the Creative Actors Workshop. Tori also enjoys reading. "I read all types of books," she says. "I like classics and I also like Jackie Collins. And I love Stephen King! I'm really into horror books."

What did Tori say when asked to describe herself? "I think I'm pretty easygoing," she divulged. "I get along with people well. My friends think I'm really funny. I like to entertain people. Not so much in being the center of attention, but I like to have fun telling jokes to my friends and stuff." If Tori had to choose one color to "describe" her personality, what would it be? Red, because it's cheerful and bright—just like Tori!

One of Tori's closest pals is Shannen Doherty. The

two spend a lot of time on and off the "Beverly Hills, 90210" set. When asked what she likes most about Shannen, Tori replied, "Probably honesty. She's the one friend I can tell anything to, or ask anything, and she'll be completely honest. We always talk and she's always there for me."

And what did Shannen have to say about her best bud, Tori? "She's very open and honest," explained Shannen. "She's there for her friends, which is a wonderful thing to find in a friend. She's really grown and come into her own as an actress, too. In general, she's just a very objective person and I like that!" Shannen also says that not many people may describe Tori as this, but nonetheless, "she's a wild girl! She has the wildest, most bizarre, driest sense of humor I've ever come across!"

The entire cast of "Beverly Hills, 90210" spends an awful lot of time together. Tori says that in the closeness of the set you quickly spot other people's odd habits—and pick up a few of your own! "I guess the weirdest is that every morning around 6 o'clock, we drink Pepsi. No one understands that!" says Tori. "And Shannen's got this huge boom box radio in her dressing room. We blast it and dance around!"

Sounds like every day is a party on the set of "Beverly Hills, 90210"!

BRIAN AUSTIN GREEN

OH NO, IT'S DAVID SILVER! If you've been a "90210" fan from the start, then you know that the new season finds fun-loving sophomore David Silver hanging with the "cool clique." When David was a freshman, he was willing to do anything to be part of the "in" crowd of upperclassmen. The popular crowd includes Kelly, Steve, Donna, Dylan, Brandon and Brenda. Brian Austin Green, who plays David, describes his character as "the annoying guy nobody wants around, but they can't get rid of him. He's trying to be popular—the trend-setting type."

When he's not playing the class clown, Brian Austin Green is just an ordinary guy.

The new season finds David chilling with the hip crew at West Beverly Hills High. He still sticks out. For instance, remember the episode when everyone is gathered around the TV set waiting for Brandon to make his acting debut? Everyone's eating popcorn. Suddenly, there is silence except for the sound of David chomping loudly and greedily on the popcorn. Everyone cracks up. David's kind of goofy, but lovable nonetheless!

Is Brian Austin Green anything at all like David Silver? Well, David likes music and so does Brian. "I'm similar to him in that I'm kind of girl-crazy, but I'm dissimilar in motives," says Brian. "I personally wouldn't do a lot of the things he does."

Brian's on the set and ready for "action."

GETTING TO THE BOTTOM OF BRI Brian Austin Green was born July 15, 1973 in Van Nuys, California. His career began at the ripe old age of 11. Brian appeared in a film by a University of Southern California graduate student. After that, Brian decided that acting was the way to go. "I was bitten by the acting bug!" says Brian. His parents, George and Joyce, were completely supportive of Brian's career decision and helped him any way they could.

Soon after his first acting stint, Brian followed up with several national television commercials and voiceovers. He made his television series debut on the CBS evening drama "Knots Landing." Brian played Brian Cunningham, Abby Ewing's (Donna Mills) son. Some of the other shows that Brian appeared in include "Bay Watch," "Highway to Heaven," "Small Wonder" and "The New Leave It To Beaver." Brian also starred in the highly-acclaimed television miniseries "Baby M," the stage production of "Ah, Wilderness!" and in the feature films "Kid," "Kickboxer II" and "An American Summer." In the latter, Brian played a Huckleberry Finn-type of character who digs surfing. That sat very well with Brian, because he loves to surf in real life! "It seemed like a huge party," he says about the filming of that movie. "We were always on the beach, where it felt like you didn't have a care in the world!"

Now at the age of 18, Brian has been acting for over seven years. He enjoys being in show business and doesn't see himself leaving the field. "I always wanted to act," says Brian. "But I would also like to try directing at some point in my career. I'd definitely like to do more feature films. I like comedy. I'd also like to do some serious dramatic stuff, too."

When asked about the drawbacks of acting, Brian could think of only one. He said that his schedule is always so back-and-forth that sometimes he has to be on the "Beverly Hills, 90210" set at sunrise and other times he can sleep until one o'clock in the afternoon!

You may not know this about Brian Austin Green, but he's also got a musical side. In fact, Brian was in a rap band called Think 2wice along with Robin Thicke

You'll be seeing more of this slightly goofy character in the second season of "Beverly Hills, 90210."

("Growing Pains'" star Alan Thicke's son) until very recently. The band split up and Brian is in the process of regrouping with some other pals. He says that in a future episode of "90210," his character may perform with a group. Says Brian with excitement, "Anyway, my character's already into music, so it'll work. I'd like to do a couple of songs with the group doing songs that we wrote. Our music is sort of like Bell Biv DeVoe."

Brian is a big fan of rap music. If you heard Brian rap, you'd know that Brian's not only a very talented actor, he also has a future as a singer, too!

Brian's musical talent goes beyond writing and singing the lyrics. "I love the drums," reveals Brian. "Jason plays the drums, too. We do a lot of talking about music and drumming on the set. It's fun!"

In fact, Brian says that his first ambition was to be a drummer, just like his dad! In addition to drumming, Brian also really enjoys dancing. In fact, during a Guess? fashion show that he and co-stars Gabrielle and Luke participated in, David did some hip-hop street moves onstage, to the delight of the audience. When it comes to slick moves, Brian Austin's got most people beat hands-down!

Brian has lots of other things to keep him busy off the set. He likes to hang out with his friends, snow ski, swim, play basketball, skateboard, go golfing, ride his bicycle, and play with his 8-year-old cat, Fluffy, and his 2-year-old Shih-Tzu, Tiko. Other faves of Brian are the animated series "The Simpsons," the films "The Breakfast Club," "Die Hard," "Back to the Future I" and "Lethal Weapon I" and "Lethal Weapon II."

Brian claims not to have a girlfriend! "But the search is always on!" he says. What does Brian look for in a gal-pal? Intelligence, a good sense of humor and a nice personality. Brian also says that this special gal would have to be someone who is fitness-conscious. Where would this cutie take his girlfriend? Probably to the funky fifties diner Ed Debevic's for a hamburger and

When he's not West Beverly Hills High's resident DJ, Brian likes to skateboard.

shake. Brian loves their food!

Well, now that you know what Brian likes, what about those things on his not-so-favorite list? Brian lists liver as his biggest dislike. He adds that he is not too keen on watching himself on television. "It's just that I can't stand watching myself," admits Brian. "I'm just really critical."

When asked what super-critical Brian considers his

best quality, he replies, "the ability to laugh at myself."
And his worst? Brian admits that he bites his nails!

IAN ZIERING

READY, SET, GO WITH STEVE! "Steve Sanders thinks he can get away with flashing a smile and buying his way out of trouble," says Ian Ziering about his "Beverly Hills, 90210" character. "He is a scammer. He tries to put things over on people!" You can bet that Ian isn't anything like Steve—except for sharing that flashy smile!

Ian says that his high school years weren't anything like those portrayed on "Beverly Hills, 90210" each week.

"Well, it's funny," begins Ian. "I grew up in West Orange, New Jersey. When we drive through the streets of Beverly Hills, I never see any kids playing on the street. You know, manicured landscapes. It's extremely beautiful...every blade of grass exactly the right height."

Ian remembers playing stickball on the street with his pals in West Orange when he was growing up. He just doesn't see stuff like that on the streets of Beverly Hills.

When it comes to comparing Ian's high school with Steve's high school, Ian says that they're like night and day. "We are using a high school down in Torrance, which is a magnificent school," says Ian. "The kids out here are a lot richer than West Orange—everybody's living in the fast lane!"

Of similarities between himself and his character, Ian jokes that they look alike.

"There are not a whole bunch of similarities between us other than that he is a caricature of me," begins Ian. "He does a lot of things that I think about, but never do. When I was younger, I was a troublemaker. The principal was always calling my house; I was getting suspended for one thing or another. But as I have grown older, with maturity, I have mellowed. But Steve Sanders has no signs of mellowing because there are no restraints on him, and he doesn't have a solid family life that's conducive to his being responsible."

Although he plays the role of stuck-up jock Steve Sanders, Ian Ziering is a really nice guy.

IAN FAX TO THE MAX! First things first—Ian Andrew Ziering pronounces his first name like "eye-an." It's even spelled phonetically on his license plate! Guess that means a lot of people mispronounce his name.

Although people are quick to spread rumors that one cast member doesn't get along with another and so on,

Ian says that everybody gets along great and there are no power tug-of-wars on the "Beverly Hills, 90210" set.

"The cast acknowledges that J Priestley, our man, is the show's quarterback, and thank God for him because he's doing a great job!" says Ian. "And there are no hostilities about that at all. I'm glad he's in the driver's seat!"

Ian says that the whole cast is very close and that everyone appreciates each other's friendship. They count on each other and maintain a sense of professionalism on the set that makes working on the show a pleasure. That doesn't mean they don't have fun! Ian and his close buds, Luke and Jason, do their share of goofing around. Luke and J nicknamed Ian the I-man or the Z-man after the copy machine character in a skit from "Saturday Night Live."

When it comes to home life, Ian says his is radically different from Steve's situation. Ian was pretty surprised when he landed the role of Hollywood honey Steve Sanders.

"They had to come east to find a California kid!" he exclaims. "I find some humor in that because I was born to a working class family. My father was a school teacher and my mom was a housewife, and I was anything but spoiled."

What are some of blue-eyed Ian's favorite things? Here's a short list: the colors red, blue and dark green; his mom's chicken parmigiana; "Catcher in the Rye" by J.D. Salinger; "The Outsiders" by S.E. Hinton; the movie "Awakenings" starring Robin Williams and Robert De Niro; "The Simpsons" TV series; the Giants football team; the group C & C Music Factory; salt water fishing; Star Trek; his dog, Coty; and actresses Christine Lahti and Meryl Streep.

Ian adores performing. His most memorable moment was when he performed on Broadway. When asked about his future goals, the I-man replied, "live to be 110!" You can bet that Ian is going to be around for quite a while!

GABRIELLE CARTERIS

ALL ABOUT ANDREA When Brandon starts settling into his new life at West Beverly Hills High, he finds his niche on the school paper. The newspaper is run by Andrea Zuckerman. Andrea is very up on social issues such as women's rights and apartheid. At first, Brandon and Andrea don't hit it off that well, because sometimes she can come on like a ton of bricks. That turns off Brandon immediately. After their initial clash, the two become closer.

Brandon finds out why Andrea is the way she is. Andrea is so determined and headstrong because she is attending West Beverly Hills High illegally. Andrea lives in the San Fernando Valley in a low-income dwelling, but uses her grandma's Beverly Hills' address so she can attend the prestigious West Beverly Hills High. She wants to go to the best school she can, so she can get the best college scholarship possible.

Gabrielle Carteris plays the intellectual Andrea. "She is a strong and stable individual who pursues what she wants by turning every obstacle into an opportunity," says Gabrielle of her "90210" character. "Andrea" is the moral voice of the show."

Gabrielle is pretty happy lately because her talents as an actress were not overlooked by the producers of "Beverly Hills, 90210." Her role as Andrea was originally intended as an ensemble regular. However, after her magnificent performances, her part was expanded. As a result, America sees a lot more of Andrea Zuckerman in every "Beverly Hills, 90210" episode.

GABBIN' WITH GABBY Hazel-eyed Gabrielle Carteris was born in Phoenix, Arizona. Her parents are divorced, and Gabrielle and her twin brother were raised in San Francisco, California, by their mom. Gabby's mom ran a successful line of clothing outlets.

Gabrielle's own sensitivity shines through her role of Andrea.

Early on, Gabrielle developed an interest in acting, dancing and pantomime. Possessing a streak of courage to go for the gusto, Gabrielle decided to leave the security of her home at the age of 14! She traveled all over Europe with a troupe of mimes and gained plenty of acting experience. Soon after, she went on to London where she studied at the Royal Academy of Dramatic Arts and the London Academy of Music and Dramatic Arts. Gabrielle says that her experiences in England were extremely valuable in laying down a firm foundation on which to build her acting career.

After her trip abroad, she returned to the States and moved to Westchester, New York, where she attended Sarah Lawrence College. Gabrielle studied theater and psychology there. Gabrielle received great reviews for her roles in the productions of "Les Liaisons Dangereuses," "The Mule & The Milky Way" and other shows.

After graduating from college, opportunities began presenting themselves to the eager-to-work Gabby. She landed roles in the off-Broadway production of "Stella," on a CBS award-winning after-school special, and in ABC's "Seasonal Differences" and "Just Between Friends." Producers of the soap "Another World" were so impressed with Gabrielle's acting achievements, they created a role for her which later developed into a series regular! That's extraordinary!

Soon after, Gabrielle started going out on Hollywood auditions. Among them was one for the two-hour pilot of a new show called "The Class of Beverly Hills" (later changed to "Beverly Hills, 90210"). After a series of callbacks and a lot of nervous anticipation, Gabby was offered the role of Andrea. She was thrilled!

Something that's very important to Gabrielle is helping those in need. While she was in college, she made a point of lending a hand at the Lexington School for the Deaf. Even now, Gabrielle is still active in helping the deaf. She also is a big supporter of environmental protection.

Gabrielle Carteris in a wild and crazy mood!

In her spare time, Gabby dabbles in writing children's stories. In the future, she hopes to publish some of her stories and also sees herself directing. Some of the performers that Gabrielle admires are Meryl Streep, Katharine Hepburn and Robert Duvall.

In her spare time, Gabrielle enjoys horseback riding, scuba diving, snow skiing, swimming, volleyball and martial arts. She also likes playing with her bird, which she calls by two names: Lucille Ball and Magilacuty. Among her likes are Japanese food, baked potatoes, jazz and blues music, and playing a good game of ten-

49

As Kelly Taylor, Jennie Garth is the leader of the pack at West Beverly Hills High.

nis. When asked what she looks for in a guy, Gabrielle replied, "Someone bright, articulate and funny."

JENNIE GARTH

THE KELLY CLIQUE Early in the series, pretty—but lethal—Kelly Taylor warned a new student at West Beverly Hills High, "You make one false move and you're history!" If you remember that line, then you probably already know that Kelly was talking to Brenda Walsh. A few episodes down the line, Kelly and her best friend Donna befriend Brenda. Bren was finally admitted into the popular clique ruled by Kelly Taylor—and boy, was she happy!

Kelly is well known for snobbery among her peers in West Beverly Hills High (especially the bumbling tag-a-long David Silver). Jennie Garth says of her character,

"I think deep down everyone can relate to Kelly—everybody has a little bit of arrogance in them."

Jennie doesn't think that there are so many differences between herself and her "Beverly Hills, 90210" character, Kelly. Jennie was also a bit of a social butterfly in high school.

"I'm never going to be an adult!" proclaims the fun-loving Jennie.

However, you can draw the line there. Jennie may look like Kelly, but they're not the same person. Kelly spends a lot of time in expensive boutiques and primping in front of a mirror. Jennie is more apt to drag a brush through her hair and head out the door to do whatever she can for the environment. Can you picture Kelly doing something like that?

GETTING STARTED Jennifer "Jennie" Garth was born on April 3, 1972 in Urbana, Illinois. She is the youngest of *seven* children! Her childhood was more about wearing jeans, cowboy boots and being down-to-earth, than wearing the newest fad to school and driving the coolest car. Blue-eyed Jennie spent her pre-teen years growing up on her family's farm. Asked about her favorite childhood memory, she replies, "My childhood was so great, that it's hard to say." When Jennie was 13 years old, her family moved to Phoenix, Arizona.

So, how exactly did pretty, blonde-haired Jennie get into acting? She sort of stumbled into it. When she was competing in a local teen beauty pageant, a former ABC-TV casting director approached her. This took Jennie by surprise. In fact, it took the casting director nearly two years to convince the country girl and her mom to make the move to Los Angeles so Jennie could actively pursue a career in acting.

Soon after they made the move, Jennie's career began taking off. Her first acting credit was a starring role with Barbara Eden in NBC's "A Brand New Life." Then Jennie starred in "Teen Angel Returns" (along with Jason Priestley) and "Just Perfect" for the Disney Channel.

Jennie also made some guest appearances on such shows as "Growing Pains" and "Circus of the Stars." In fact, in this year's "Circus of the Stars" extravaganza, Jennie is doing an act called The Web. Her "90210" co-star Gabrielle Carteris is performing on the trapeze.

Jennie's biggest break was landing the role of snobby snubber Kelly Taylor on "Beverly Hills, 90210." Jennie says that the character is a lot of fun to play because it's so different from her own personality.

"Living in a small town and coming from a very tight and close family instilled a lot of standards that I need to live up to," says Jennie. That's probably why she's so passionate about saving the environment and protecting animal rights. Makes a lot of sense for a gal who says her first ambition was "to be happy and free."

Kelly is a rich brat, and that couldn't be farther away from a description of the real Jennie. Her co-star, Luke Perry, describes Jennie with one word: "sweetness." "I am from Ohio and she's from Illinois," says Luke. "We are both farm people."

Jennie spends the majority of her free time with her close friends or just hanging out with her family. Whenever she can, Jennie likes to play with her dog Sasha, listen to the Rolling Stones and eat Mexican food. Currently, Jennie resides in Sherman Oaks, California, where she recently purchased her own house. Jennie even helped her parents purchase a house, as well!

Soft-spoken Jennie's future in acting is looking brighter than ever! This past September, Jennie was chosen as one of ten "Female Stars of Tomorrow" by Bob Hope for one of his TV specials. You'll most likely be seeing a lot of Jennie not only on "Beverly Hills, 90210," but on other television shows and the big screen!

CAROL POTTER & JAMES ECKHOUSE

MEET MOM & DAD Cindy and Jim Walsh are Brandon and Brenda's very concerned and caring parents.

"Cindy Walsh is a mother who is always there for her children," says Carol Potter of her "Beverly Hills, 90210" character. "She's a very stable, down-to-earth person amid all the glitz and hype of Beverly Hills."

What about Dad, the accountant? He's a father who is striving to keep his family as close as possible in a drastically different environment. He wants to give his family the best possible life, while maintaining their midwestern values.

Whenever Brenda and Brandon have a problem, their parents are there for them. Cindy and Jim listen and give advice. The other kids on "90210" aren't as lucky—their parents are always out and about, at times ignoring them altogether.

Sometimes, Jim and Cindy Walsh even give their kids' chums advice. Remember when Dylan's mom comes back into his life? She bonds with Cindy and asks why Dylan is acting so hostile. Cindy tells the worried mother that she's trying too hard too fast to be Dylan's mom. That episode of "Beverly Hills, 90210" provided the audience with Dylan's view and his mom's as well. That helps teens understand where their parents are coming from and vice versa. As always, communication is the key.

IN REALITY Carol Potter, who plays Mrs. Walsh, is a native New Yorker who was raised in Tenafly, New Jersey. She studied drama while attending high school. She enjoyed acting, but majored in psychology when she went to Radcliffe College. After she graduated from Radcliffe, she decided "you only live once" and that she was going to go after her dream. She packed her bags and headed for New Haven, Connecticut, where she worked at the prestigious Williamstown Theatre Festival. Her first road production was "The Effect of Gamma Rays on Man in the Moon Marigolds" with Shelley Winters and Teresa Wright. Carol's first real break was when she landed the role of Judith Hastings in the long-running Broadway show "Gemini." She moved to

Brian Austin Green, Ian Ziering and Douglas Emerson—co-stars in the first season of "Beverly Hills, 90210"—wave the Fox banner.

California in 1981 when she landed a role on the short-lived series "Today's FBI." After that, she landed the role of Cindy Walsh on "Beverly Hills, 90210." Most of her free time is spent raising her three-year-old son, Christopher. Any time she has free, she spends volunteering with various charities.

James Eckhouse is a native of Chicago, Illinois, who was raised, in part, in England. James was always interested in the sciences and went on to attend M.I.T. He studied physics and biology with the hope of eventually going on to medical school. After two years, however, Jim decided that his real passion was for acting, so he left. He started pursuing a career in theater and performed in various works at the Public Theatre, Playwrights Horizons, the Williamstown Theatre Festival and the Manhattan Theatre Club. Jim's television credits include "Matlock," "Equal Justice," "thirtysomething" and "Capital News." He also starred in the Movies-of-the-Week "In the Best Interest of the Child" and "Will There Really be a Morning." Jim's motion picture roles include "Cocktail," with Tom Cruise, "Trading Places," "Defending Your Life" and "Fat Man and Little Boy." When he's not playing the aboveboard Jim Walsh, he's busy playing real dad to his own sons. He also enjoys carpentry, sailing, tennis and reading a good book.

DOUGLAS EMERSON

ONCE UPON A TIME Remember Scott Scott? He was the level-headed sidekick of David Silver. In the new season opener you probably noticed that Scott was not listed in the credits. That's because his character was written off the show. Scott was the bright, but socially-innocent freshman at West Beverly Hills High. "Scott is just your typical freshman trying to fit in, but he has enough sense to know that you can stay clean and still have fun," Douglas has said of his "90210" character.

Is Douglas sad his role of Scott was written off the show? Of course he is! He really enjoyed working on "Beverly Hills, 90210." He says that it was a great cast to work with and he learned a lot this past year. Douglas says that the best part of acting is "the experience of getting to work with people you admire." You can bet that the cast of "Beverly Hills, 90210" misses Douglas, too! But he sees this as a time to move on to the next acting project. Look for Douglas in other projects coming up soon. If there is one thing he likes to do it is act!

Although Doug Emerson's role as Scott Scott has been eliminated, program fans will never forget his contribution to the first season of "Beverly Hills, 90210."

ALL ABOUT DOUG Douglas Edward Emerson was born on October 5, 1974 in Glendale, California. Douglas currently resides in the San Fernando Valley. He has two brothers, Toby and Curtis, and two sisters, Wendy and Rachel. His entire family has been very supportive of his career—especially his mom, Ann.

Douglas is no newcomer to acting! He started his show business career at the young age of 4, in a television commercial. Now, his acting resumé includes over 60 television commercials! He's also made appearances on "The Wonder Years," "Mr. Belvedere," "Night Court," "Small Wonder," "General Hospital" and "Highway to Heaven." Also, Doug was a series regular on both "One to Grow On" and "Herbie the Love Bug." His screen credits include "The Blob," "Blob Slam," "Police Academy" and "Million Dollar Mystery."

On the personal side, Doug says that his dream car is a Saab 900 Turbo. In fact, Doug likes all kinds of cars and keeps up on the latest models and technological advances. If he was stranded on a deserted island, what would food would he choose to live on? Macaroni and cheese, and blueberry muffins. He absolutely adores them!

Douglas spends a good part of his free time volunteering with the Rainbow Group III, a group of young stars who visit kids who are suffering from cancer. Douglas is very aware that not all of us are fortunate and he lends a hand whenever he can to the needy.

So, what does Doug Emerson like in a girl? "Good personality and a sense of humor, and she has to be able to tell me what she's thinking and how she's feeling," says blond-haired, blue-eyed Doug. Where would he take a girlfriend? To a formal dance or other function, because he just loves wearing a tuxedo. And you'd better believe he looks gorgeous in a tux!

Doug Emerson, Ian Ziering, and Brian Austin Green are off the set goofing around between their scenes.

On the set . . .
of one of
today's top
TV dramas.

ADMINISTRATION
OFFICE

STUDENT
CONGRESS
* Tue.
Little
theatre

CHAPTER 3

"BEVERLY HILLS, 90210" TIDBITS

JASON ON ACTING

"I've never been satisfied with any performance I've ever given. It forces me to improve, which I think is the most important thing."

DAREDEVIL LUKE

Luke likes the challenge of doing things that scare him. Once, he jumped a motorcycle over two Volkswagen cars! That's daring!

GABRIELLE ON ANDREA

"The stuff the writers have had me doing for the last few episodes is great. Andrea's blossoming into a really full person."

SHANNEN ABOUT THE SHOW'S SUCCESS

"I think it's because it's the first show that really portrays teenagers as having intelligence. It really deals with controversial issues and appeals to a huge group of all ages. I mean, anybody can watch the show."

TORI SHARES SHANNEN'S SECRET NO. 1

"Here's a good one. She has three obnoxious pet doves! They coo all the time and get feathers everywhere! Shannen has to vacuum about a million times a day. I'm always saying, 'Why do you have these birds?' And she's just like, 'I don't know.' I guess she just loves animals!"

DOWN-TO-EARTH J

Jason says that he has plenty of values that he tries to stay true to. His only fear is that he ends up sounding arrogant or preachy.

WHAT BRIAN LIKES ABOUT ACTING

"I get to be someone other than Brian Green. All of a sudden, you're a totally new person, living a whole other life!"

Gabrielle and Brian Austin were guests at the Noxzema Extraordinary Teen Contest and awarded the winner her prize!

IAN ON HIS CHARACTER, STEVE

"My character really doesn't know any boundaries. How wrong is wrong? How much right is right? And are there consequences?"

LUKE ON IAN

"Ian was on 'Guiding Light.' I went to New York to test for a part on another soap and Ian was there, too—we were competing against each other for the same part. And I thought, 'What is he, greedy? He already has a job, he wants two?' But I found out he wasn't really getting much to do on 'Guiding Light.' Eventually, they made his part bigger on that show, which is a good thing because he's a good actor."

TORI WOULD LOVE TO MEET...

Tori really admires actors James Spader and Johnny Depp.

THE MOVIE THAT STUCK TO LUKE LIKE GLUE

"'Cool Hand Luke'—I saw my name on TV! That was the best. I'd never seen it in writing before. I must've watched that movie 50 times!"

SHANNEN ABOUT WHO'S CUTER—JASON OR LUKE?

"Umm ... Jason has those eyes, and Luke has that scar. And they're both very cute. Luke is very skinny, Jason's shorter. You know, they both are very good-looking guys—and they're great to work with!"

LUKE'S PHILOSOPHY

"I don't prize possessions; I prize people."

TORI'S DAD LAYS DOWN THE LAW

"We trust Tori and Randy," says big-time producer Aaron Spelling of his kids. "We never tell them what they can watch. They understand. Tori was coming to the set when she was five years old. She knows that blood on TV isn't real."

BRIAN "KID" GREEN

In the flick "Kid," Brian Austin Green played Louie, an aspiring heavy metal guitar player.

SHANNEN'S BEAUTY SECRETS

"I wash my face twice a day and follow up with an astringent and a light moisturizer. I try not to eat junk food or greasy foods."

GABRIELLE'S IN SYNCH WITH ANDREA

"Everything that I like about Andrea is a thing I like about myself. My mother said that every generation has the responsibility to be better than the last. I believe that."

JENNIE'S BIGGEST LIKES

Trees, dogs and good people! Sounds like all the makings of a wonderful picnic!

LUKE ON THE ENVIRONMENT

"I am a supporter of Greenpeace and a strong believer in taking an active role to preserve all aspects of our environment."

WHAT IAN DOES TO RELAX

For fun, Ian likes to play Nintendo, but for total relaxation, Ian gazes at the fish swimming around in his aquarium.

IAN & HIS DOG

"There's a park in California where you're allowed to let your dog run without a leash. After 3 o'clock, there's about two to three hundred dogs there. It's a sight to see."

FINAL WORD

Now, you can consider yourself officially hip to the zip! In order to stay that way though you'd better tune in to "Beverly Hills, 90210" each and every week. There are new characters popping in and out of the show all the time. Remember the season opener, when Christine Elise starred as the new girl in school, Emily Valentine. Dylan and Brandon both fell for her! That was a pretty exciting episode! So, keep on the ball and don't miss a show!